Things Can

Only Get

Verse

A Collection of

Humorous Poems

By Viv Wade.

Contents

The Bore

He just talks on and on...

The sight of him fills me with dread,
I wish I was elsewhere, or dead.
I don't care what he has to say,
I just want him to go away.

I've heard his stories all before,
At least a thousand times or more,
Although I've not been keeping score.
His droning voice just makes me snore.

He'd talk the hind legs off a horse,
And then the head, for second course.
I watch his mouth open and close,
And feel my brain begin to doze.

He doesn't seem to pause for breath,
He makes me wish that I was deaf.
I'm sure he thinks he fascinates,
I grit my teeth, his tone just *grates*.

He loves the sound of his own voice,
He doesn't give me any choice,
He tells each tale right to the end,
I wish he'd find another friend.

His speech is all in monotone.
Why doesn't he leave me alone?
He pours his drivel in my ears,
It really does bore me to tears.

The conversation's not two-way,
He won't hear what I have to say,
For if I try to say a word,
He shouts, so that I can't be heard.

It's really just a monologue,
Why doesn't he go write a blog
And post it on the internet?
No one would read it, you can bet.

If I was an insomniac,
I'd tape his voice, then play it back.
I'm sure his speech could outperform
A sleeping pill, or chloroform.

We all know someone who's a bore,
Who talks and talks, for ever more.
But if you've thought, and don't know who,
It may be that the bore is YOU!

A Virtual Life

Social networking can be so engrossing, that real life just passes you by...

I have 500 Facebook friends!
An online social life.
They 'like' the things I share,
They never give me any strife.
I've never met them face to face,
What difference does that make?
Though no one gives me Christmas gifts,
Or makes me birthday cake.

I've loads of Twitter followers,
I tweet all night and day,
With strangers often re-tweeting
The things I have to say.
It keeps me very busy,
My whole life I must compress,
Into just one hundred and forty characters,
Or less.

I took a cruise-ship holiday,
And sailed all round about.
I posted loads of selfies,
To show off my sun-tanned pout.
I saw some lovely scenery,
All through my smartphone lens.
Uploaded it on Instagram,
To brag to all my friends.

I had a lovely Chinese meal,
While dining all alone.
I felt the need to share it,
And got out my mobile phone.
I took a pic, uploaded it,
And captioned it in bold
On all the social networks,
While my dinner grew stone cold.

We're living in the perfect time
For making loads of friends.
Communicating round the world,
The chatting never ends.
So what if you can't shake their hand,
Or share a warm embrace?
That's the way we live now,
We're the Virtual Human Race.

The Self-Service Checkout

5 012345 678900

Whatever happened to customer service?

Of all the machinery man has invented,
There is one contraption that drives me demented!
The most useless gadget that I've ever seen,
Is the supermarket self-checkout machine.

Once, nice checkout ladies would say, "How d'you do?"
And help to pack all of your shopping for you.
But they're being replaced by those robot-voiced scanners,
Who just shout at you, and don't have any manners.

The first thing it does is weigh my shopping bag,
To check I'm not shop-lifting, like some old lag.
If my bag seems heavy, it calls an assistant,
Its voice is accusing, so loud and persistent.

So I stand there and wait while someone checks my bag,
To ensure that I'm not making off with some swag.

Then once the assistant decides I'm not scamming,
I start the laborious process of scanning.

I search for a barcode on each tin and pack,
I look on the front, and the side, and the back.
I frown when the barcode cannot be located,
And call the assistant – I feel so frustrated!
She saunters on over, as slow as she's able,
And points to the barcode, hid under a label.
She looks at me like I'm a silly old fool,
I grit my teeth, trying not to lose my cool.

The first item I scan comes up with the wrong price,
Thirty-four ninety-nine, for a small bag of rice!
With one barcode the scanner refuses to beep,
Has the thing broken down, or just fallen asleep?
On some baked beans, the dratted thing beeps at me twice.
I'm being double charged, and that's not very nice!

Then just as I'm scanning and bagging the bread,
It shouts out the phrase that most fills me with dread.
"UNEXPECTED ITEM IN THE BAGGING AREA!"
I'd rather have flu, or a dose of malaria
Than to hear the machine shouting that well-worn phrase,
While security guards hold me fast in their gaze.

So listen up, all of you big supermarkets,
To hell with your profits, and yearly sales targets.
Unless your machines are polite and efficient,
I'll grow my own produce – become self-sufficient!

The Hangover

Never again...

We went out to our local pub, a jolly atmosphere,
With wines and spirits of all kinds, and twenty types of beer.
I tried to sample all of them, it only seemed polite,
But now I wish I hadn't, 'cause I really feel like shite!

I was so full of life and joy while I was there, imbibing,
But now I look like death warmed up, I'm only just surviving.
My head thumps like a steam hammer, my brain is slow and thick,
And if I try to move, I feel like I want to be sick.

I'm normally an atheist, religion I've not found.
And yet I prayed, "God, help me!", as the room spun round and round.
I called him from the bathroom, down that great white telephone,
And groaned, "Oh Lord, I'm dying!" But I don't think he was home.

What was that funny green liqueur that someone made me drink?
It looked like something you might use to clear a bunged-up sink!

I thought it tasted rather nice, and so I drank some more,
But after half a bottle, I was flat out on the floor.

My memories of last night are a little vague and hazy,
Was I singing on the tables – or am I going crazy?
I'm normally reserved and shy, but when I've had a few,
I think I am Beyoncé live on stage at the O2.

The evening ended in a blur – how did I get back home?
And how did I end up in bed with someone's garden gnome?
And why is there a donkey outside, by the garden shed?
Perhaps I couldn't find a cab, and rode him home instead.

From now on, I will promise, I'm not drinking anymore,
I'm turning teetotal, once I can get up off the floor.
So clear my liquor cabinet, throw out all of the grog,
No wait, before you do – I'll have a quick 'hair of the dog'!

The Liar

You can tell when he's lying, his lips move...

Years ago, I had a boyfriend
Who liked to brag and boast.
When talking of his salary,
He'd say he earned the most.
Yet when we went to dinner,
He'd forget to bring his money.
"Oh, silly me!" he'd laugh,
Although I didn't find it funny.

He said he was a DJ,
In demand in all the clubs.
He only had two records,
'Hitler's Speeches' and 'N-Dubz'.
He once gave me a diamond ring,
The biggest rock I'd seen!
But the stone dissolved in water,
And my finger turned bright green.

He said he owned a red Lotus,
He'd bought it in Milan.
I only ever saw him drive
A rusty, three-wheeled van.
He said he had a penthouse suite
In Paris, near the Seine.
The only place we ever went
Was Bognor, in the rain.

He said he'd been a footballer,
Played the Premier League.
Yet when I saw him kick a ball,
He fainted with fatigue.
He also said he was
A secret agent in disguise,
I realised that all he'd said
Was just a pack of lies.

I told him he was dumped,
For being a false, deceitful person.
He said he didn't care,
He had a date with Elle McPherson.
I shoved his fake designer clothes
In his mock Gucci bag,
And told him he could go elsewhere
To lie, and boast, and brag.

The last I heard of him,
He had fulfilled his dream ambition.
He now gets paid for telling lies,
He is a politician.

Diane's Disastrous Date

Diane thought the date was going well, until...

Diane heaved a loud sigh as she picked up her ringing phone.
She almost hadn't answered, pretended she wasn't home.
Her mom rang twenty times a day to bend her daughter's ear,
(She was the type of woman who has verbal diarrhoea.)

"Hello, Diane," a manly voice came smoothly down the line,
"I thought I'd ring and ask you out, if you are free sometime?
If you would like, I'll pick you up and take you out tonight.
We'll go to that new bistro in the High Street, that alright?"

Diane was stunned – she recognised the voice of Michael Kerr!
She'd always fancied him, but didn't think he'd noticed her.
"OK!" she squeaked, then cleared her throat. "Please pick me up at seven!"
"Will do," said Mike, and rang off. Diane raised her eyes to heaven.
"Oh, thank you, God!" she said out loud, "You've answered all my prayers!"
"But what to wear?" she panicked, as she hurried up the stairs.

Diane looked in her wardrobe, but her clothes did not inspire.
She needed something ravishing, that Michael would admire.
Before she closed the door, she spotted something at the bottom.
A dress she'd bought and never worn, one she'd almost forgotten.

She pulled it out, and tried it on, and looked at her reflection.
It really was a gorgeous frock, sartorial perfection!
In deepest red, with plunging neck, and clever bodice tucks,
It pushed bits up, and pulled bits in – she looked a million bucks!
Diane knew that she looked just right, this was the perfect dress
To wear on her hot date tonight, she knew she would impress.

At seven, she was waiting for her gallant beau to knock,
Her make-up and her hair done, and new shoes to match the frock.
Then just as she began to fear that Michael wouldn't show,
He rapped upon the door. She gasped, "He's here, it's time to go!"

He drove her to the restaurant, beneath the moonlit skies,
And as he parked the car, he turned and gazed into her eyes.
He told her she looked beautiful as they sat at the table.
He looked so very handsome, like a modern day Clark Gable.

The evening went so perfectly, they talked, and laughed, and smiled.
He couldn't keep his eyes off her, he clearly was beguiled.
A violin serenaded them, Mike gave Diane a rose,
And as he paid the bill, she said, "I'll just powder my nose."

"I can't believe my luck!" she thought, while seated on the toilet.
"This really is the perfect date, there's not a thing to spoil it.
I'm sure he'll ask me out again, tonight is just the start.
I really think I am the girl to capture Michael's heart!"

She washed her hands, and left the room, but as she crossed the floor,
From somewhere close behind her, she could hear a loud guffaw.
Another laugh, and then a giggle, someone gave a shout!
Diane could not help wondering what they all laughed about.
She turned around to find the cause of all the diners' snickers,
And glancing down, she saw her dress was tucked up in her knickers!

She blushed bright red! She knew this would haunt her mind for weeks.
How could this have happened – she'd shown everyone *both cheeks!*
And worse than that, for trailed across the bistro, from the loo,
A length of toilet paper, which had stuck onto her shoe!
She looked across at Michael, hoped he had not seen her plight,
But he was staring straight at her, his lips were closed up tight.
She quickly pulled her dress down, took the paper off her shoe,
As Michael said, "I think I'd better take you home, don't you?"

They drove back home in silence, Michael never made a sound.
Diane wished she could disappear, just vanish underground.
They parked outside her house, she said, "Shall I expect your call?"
He said, "I wouldn't hold your breath, there is no point at all.
This must be the most mortifying evening I have had,
And if we never meet again, I will be very glad.
You made me look a laughing stock, in such a public place.
I thought you were a cool chick, but you're really a disgrace!"

Diane stared back at Michael, saying, "You thought I was cool?
Well, I thought you were too, but you are just a pompous fool!
And there's another thing – here, you can keep your rotten rose!"
And as she spoke, she grasped the flower, and shoved it up his nose.

She got out of the car, went in the house, and slammed the door,
Then sobbed her broken heart out, lying on the bedroom floor.
And early the next morning, when her crying was all done,
She went down to the convent, and she enrolled as a nun.

Mother's Magic Medicine

A cure for all known ills...

When I was a little kid,
If I wasn't feeling well,
My mother made a potion
That gave off an awful smell.

I don't know what ingredients
She used to put in it,
But after just one spoonful,
I would soon be fighting fit!

It healed my gran's lumbago,
And my grandad's dodgy hip,
It got rid of Dad's headache,
And he only had a sip.

It eased my brother's acne,
And his tendency to blush,
It cured my sister's stutter,
And a nasty case of thrush.

It wasn't just a medicine,
It shifted stubborn stains,
Annihilated woodworm,
And it even unblocked drains!

She kept it in a lead lined flask,
I know that might sound drastic,
But when she used a pop bottle,
It melted through the plastic!

I wish my mother was still here,
To make some of her potion.
I'd have a go myself,
But I just haven't got a notion.

I wish I had the recipe,
It could bring untold wealth,
Or failing that, I wish they did it
On the National Health.

<u>Wedding Planning</u>

A wedding takes a lot of organising...

We have to plan our wedding day - the best day of our lives!
I'm sure I'll make you happier than all your former wives.
I'm glad we're in agreement that we want to keep it small,
To start our married life in debt would not be wise at all.

So let's start with the guest list first, we must keep it select,
(Although we can't avoid asking your mother, I expect.)
There's my parents and my brother, and sister Sue of course,
(Although she'll spoil the photos, she looks *so* much like a horse!)
There's Uncle Ted, and Aunty Pat, and Cousin Cyril too,
No wait – I think I heard he'd emigrated to Peru.
There's Grandad Bob, and Nana Jess, And Uncle Terry Finement,
(Who's now called *Aunt Teresa*, since his gender reassignment.)

Now, what about your brothers, dear? You know they always fight!
You must make sure they don't do too much drinking on the night.

We won't ask Cousin Geraldine, you know she'll only spoil it,
Remember Katy's wedding, when she passed out in the toilet?
We must ask Uncle David – don't forget, he's stinking rich!
He'll bring a lovely gift, (it's just a shame his wife's a bitch.)

Now, what about our work colleagues? I'll have to ask my boss,
And if I don't invite all of the sales team, they'll be cross.
There's Carol on reception, and Annette from Personnel.
(If I ask her, I'll have to ask the other twelve as well.)

Now, please don't ask your boss, you know he is an *awful* bore,
I met him at your Christmas do, he almost made me snore!
In fact, all of your colleagues are a bit beyond the pale,
(I think they've escaped from a mental hospital - or jail!)

Now what about your friends? Well, I suppose we must ask *some*.
(I'll forget to post their invites, and hope that they won't come.)
Now all my college friends *must* come, they're such a charming bunch!
The sort who know which cutlery is which, when out for lunch.
Whereas your old school buddies are a proper load of mingers,
(They're bound to pick their dinner up, and eat it with their fingers!)

We must ask Roger Huntingdon, if he's home from the army,
On second thoughts, we'd better not – his missus is quite barmy!
We're not inviting Emma Jane, I hope that you agree,
I'm not having a woman there who's prettier than me!
It's *my* wedding day, *I* should be the most stunning woman there!
And I will be, if an expert does my make-up, nails and hair.

Now what about your offspring from your previous liaisons?
You'd have to calm them down a bit - try Valium, the strong ones!

23

It's best not to invite them both, if you'll take my advice,
(The big one is a biter, and the little one has lice!)
I don't want them as bridesmaids, as I don't think I could hack it,
(Unless their bridesmaids' dresses fasten up like a straitjacket!)

Now that's the guest list sorted, so what else is left to plan?
My wedding dress, of course, a suit for you, and your best man.
The church to hold the wedding, and a place for the reception,
I dread to think what it will cost us, far too much to mention!
We must compile a gift list, and design the invitations,
Perhaps some really tasteful ones, embroidered with carnations.
A band to play the music, so the wedding guests can dance,
And someone to take photographs, to capture our romance.

A chauffeur-driven limousine to take me to the church,
They must arrive on time, so I don't leave you in the lurch!
And then there is the wedding cake, and catering to do,
I never knew that weddings took so much planning, did you?
I'm getting such a headache, there's too much to think about!
It's making me think twice about it all, I'm filled with doubt...

Let's tear this wedding list in two, and throw it in the bin.
A wedding's too much hassle – let's shack-up and live in sin!

The Actress

In the world of acting, looks are important...

Suzy was an actress.
She had trod the boards for years,
Though she hadn't had the most
Successful of careers.
She only got the minor roles
In small production plays,
Yet still she dreamed that Hollywood
Would call, one of these days.

She'd done a bit of TV work,
Though mostly playing corpses,
And 'woman waiting for a bus'
In *Only Fools and Horses*.

The problem was the way she looked,
She knew that was the case.
To be a star in Hollywood,
You had to have 'The Face'.

An actress must be beautiful
To be a movie star,
And have the kind of boobs
That still look good without a bra.
You needed to look young and slim
To make it in L.A.
So Suzy knew what she must do
To make things go her way.

She'd go and have some work done
On her body, and her face,
So when she went to castings
She would not look out of place.
She found a plastic surgeon
Who would do it on the cheap,
He said he'd worked on Aniston,
And Cher, and Meryl Streep.

He said he'd give her Winslet's eyes and nose,
And Jolie's lips,
With legs like Scarlett Johansson,
And Sandra Bullock's hips.
With boobs like Pammie Anderson,
And Emma Watson's bum,
He guaranteed when he was done
The film offers would come!

She checked into the clinic,
And the surgeon set to work.
He botoxed round her forehead,
And he gave her chin a twerk.
He plumped her cheeks with implants,
And pumped filler in her lips,
He filled her boobs with silicone,
And sucked fat from her hips.

He lifted up her face,
So all her wrinkles disappeared,
Then stuck veneers on all her teeth,
And lasered off her beard.
A bum lift, and a tummy tuck,
And all the work was done.
She woke up wrapped in bandages,
And felt groggy and numb.
It took a while till all the cuts
And excisions were healed.
Then she removed the bandages -
Her new look was revealed!

She stared at her reflection,
And it almost made her swoon.
Her face looked like the back-end
Of a beaten up baboon!
Her lips looked like an inner tube,
With teeth bizarrely white,
Her face all taut and shiny,
Oh, she really looked a sight!

Her boobs were like two beach balls,
And her legs looked like two twigs,
Her eyes were like cats' bum-holes,
And her nose looked like a pig's.

Fat tears rolled down her swollen cheeks,
She looked just like a freak!
She turned the mirror to the wall,
And stayed in for a week.
She wished she'd never had the op,
She looked so fake and weird.
And all her dreams of Hollywood
Completely disappeared.

She thought her life was ruined,
Yet it's all worked out just fine -
She's starring in a remake of
The Bride of Frankenstein!

The Writer's Lament

This is the first poem I ever wrote. I started off writing short stories, and joined an internet writing site where writers can post their work and have it reviewed by others. Unfortunately, I found I wasn't getting many reviews, as it seemed most of the people on the site were only willing to review poetry. I wrote this poem in an attempt to reach out to those people!

I always thought I'd like to write
A bestseller or two,
So I resolved to have a go,
And see what I could do.

I got my trusty laptop out,
Placed it on the table,
Plugged it in to charge it up –
And tripped over the cable.

I scratched my head, and paced about,
While thinking of a plot,
Till finally an idea came!
So I gave it a shot.

I sat down and began to type,
The words came thick and fast,
I didn't want to stop
Lest inspiration didn't last.

I didn't pause for anything,
The outside world forgotten.
I didn't put the bins out,
And my fruit bowl all went rotten.

I didn't stop for food or sleep,
I did not want to shirk.
I only had a crate of wine –
Well, writing's thirsty work!

The dust grew thick upon the shelf,
The laundry went undone.
My husband packed his bags
And emigrated to the sun.

And still I sat and typed away,
Till at last it was done.
And then when I got up,
I realised my bum was numb!

I read what I had written,
And decided it was time,
To set it free, out in the world,
This little tale of mine.

I googled on the internet,
And found a writing site.
I posted what I'd written,
Then I prayed with all my might.

I waited for the words of praise
My efforts must attract.
I waited all that day,
And all week after, that's a fact.

But I got no reviews,
No, not a solitary one.
I slumped across my laptop,
For my urge to write had gone.

Oh, what's the point of writing,
If no one wants to read?
So I turned off my laptop.
It made my poor heart bleed!

Maybe someone did read it,
But they didn't leave a note,
To tell me what their feelings were
About the words I wrote.

So if you read a piece you like,
Please do stop and say.
It won't take you long,
Yet it will make the writer's day!

And if someone reviews your work,
Please do be polite;
You should review a piece of theirs –
Even if it's shite!

A Funny Age

Clothes shopping is a minefield when you're over 40...

It's tricky buying clothes these days,
I'm at a funny age!
I'm too old for a mini-skirt,
Although they're all the rage.
I'd like to wear a sparkly dress,
To make me feel all glam,
But would it only make me look
Like mutton dressed as lamb?

If I dress all in leopard print,
Will I look hip and smart?
Or will I just look desperate?
A lonely, sad old tart.

If I wear leather trousers,
Will I look sexy and cool?
Or will people just think I am
An absurd, ageing fool.

There are lots of celebrities
Who look good for their age,
I've seen them in the magazines,
They smile from every page.
But they've all got a stylist,
And a surgeon on speed-dial,
A trainer, and a dentist
For that perfect, veneered smile.
I can't compete with them,
I haven't got that sort of money.
I tried Madonna's hairstyle,
But it just made me look funny.

To hell with those young models
In the fashion magazines!
All posing in their skimpy tops,
And posh designer jeans.
I'm going to wear what I like,
Who cares what people think!
Blue platform shoes, red hotpants,
And my hair dyed shocking pink!

I'm too young for a twin-set,
And elasticated trews,
I'm not ready for blue-rinsed hair,
And frumpy, laced-up shoes.

Why should I look 'appropriate',
With hair up in a bun?
I'm not old yet.
Let's get dolled up, and go out and have fun!

Flatulent Freddy's Flying Machine

Wind powered whimsy...

Freddy saw an advert for a flying competition,
"Build a homemade aeroplane – that must be your mission!
You should construct a plane that has not been flown before,
Capable of flying for at least an hour or more.
First prize is a holiday in an exotic place."
Fred thought he would have a go, and try to win the race!

He went down to his tool shed, and had a look around,
To see what he could find that might get him off the ground.
He found a shopping trolley, and a few old bits of wood,
An engine off a lawn mower – yes, that might be some good!
With screws and nails, and nuts and bolts, he fastened them together,
Some old tarpaulin for a roof, to keep away the weather.
Fred thought that he had built a plane in which to win the race.
He couldn't keep a cheesy grin from creeping round his face!

When the contest day arrived, Freddy loaded his machine
Onto his brother's pick-up truck, and drove it to the scene.
He arrived at the aerodrome, and waited at the start,
Along with four contestants who were also taking part.
When the starting pistol fired, Freddy tried to start the plane.
Alas, the engine wouldn't work! Poor Fred cried out in pain!
The other planes were well away, with Fred stuck at the start.
He felt a nervous rumble – and let out a massive *FART!*
(He'd had a Three Bean Curry for his tea the night before.)
He farted once again – and his plane shot up off the floor!

Fred farted like a motorbike! The plane flew swift and fast.
He hoped his Three Bean Curry gas was strong enough to last!
He flew round for an hour, left the others far behind,
With thoughts of winning first place uppermost in Freddy's mind.
The other planes all lost their power, landing one by one,
While Fred still zoomed around the field – he knew the race was won!

He landed on the airstrip, and he climbed out of the plane.
His bottom let out one last *trump* – a victory refrain!
The organisers came across to shake Fred by the hand,
They said, "Congratulations, Fred! Your little plane is grand!"
They asked what powered Freddy's plane to fly in such a hurry,
He said, "It runs on natural gas – from Mother's Three Bean Curry!"

The first prize of the holiday was handed out to Fred.
He didn't go there in his plane – he flew Virgin instead.

ATISHOO!

That foul pestilence...

I've come down with another cold!
My husband is to blame.
He came down with it on Monday,
So now I've done the same.
I know that when you're married
You should share your goods and wealth,
But his germs are one thing
I wish he'd keep all to himself.

My head is full of cotton wool,
My nose runs like a tap,
My throat's as rough as sandpaper,
I really feel like crap!

My body aches from head to toe,
I'm in a lot of pain.
I feel like I am dying,
But I'm not one to complain.

I've dosed myself with Lemsip,
Got some Strepsils for my throat,
To stop myself from shivering,
I'm sleeping in my coat.
I've rubbed some Vick's all over,
It is *such* a soothing balm.
I exude so much vapour
I've set off the smoke alarm!

Because my nose is blocked,
I didn't sleep a wink last night.
Air rattled up my left nostril,
And whistled down my right.
I'm not going to work,
Though they'll be cross if I'm not there,
But to spread this round the office -
That just *would not* be fair!

I always meet those people
Who say "Here's what you should do,
Just take some echinacea,
And you'll never have the flu!"
While others swear by garlic,
Or red onion with honey,
Or horseradish - I've tried them all,
So why's my nose still runny?

We're living in a golden age
Of science and invention,
Advancements in technology
Too numerous to mention.
But listen, all you scientists,
If I may make so bold,
If you're so bloody clever,
Then please, *cure the common cold!*

Dieting Dilemma

A moment on the lips, a lifetime on the hips...

I'm trying to lose weight.
It's really rather hard!
I felt that I should try,
My thighs had turned to lard.

First I tried to cut out carbs,
That made me quite frustrated.
Although it helps you lose weight,
It makes you constipated!

Next I tried a low fat diet -
Involved a lot of grilling.
The meals were quite tasty,
But they weren't very filling.

Then I tried the Slim Fast plan,
Replacing meals with shakes.
But they left me so hungry,
I ate a load of cakes!

Next I tried Weight Watchers,
Counting calories, you see.
But I ate my allowance
Before I'd had my tea!

Then I tried a fibre diet,
It's *so* good for your heart.
But eating all those sprouts and beans
Really makes you *fart!*

Next I tried the juice diet,
I drank nothing but juice.
Spent so long in the bathroom,
I felt like a recluse!

Oh, why does our society
Demand that we be thin?
I've had enough of dieting,
I think I'll pack it in!

I just want to enjoy my life,
And never mind my size.
My scales are going in the bin...
Now, pass me those pork pies!

Different Skills

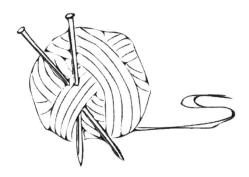

Everyone is good at something...

My grandma was a knitter,
How her needles used to fly!
You couldn't sit too close,
Or you might get one in the eye!
She'd knit me a new jumper,
Then when I grew out of that,
She'd pull it all undone,
To knit a new scarf, and a hat.

My mother was a dressmaker,
A seamstress of great skill.
When I needed a new frock,
She would set to, with a will.
She'd fetch the spare room curtains,
And her old sewing machine,
Then stitch me a new dress
That made me look just like a queen!

My father was a carpenter,
He had a way with wood.
He'd take old, broken furniture,
And mend, and make it good.
He carved a fine oak toilet seat,
It took him quite a while.
At least when it was finished,
We could all sit down in style!

I don't possess my forebears' skills,
With cloth, or wool, or wood.
The only thing that I can do
That turns out any good,
Is write a silly poem,
In a droll, light-hearted style.
If that's not very practical,
At least it makes you smile!

<u>Wasp!</u>

I don't like wasps...

The wasp is a malicious creature,
Who has not one redeeming feature,
He'll sting you without reason.
Autumn is his busiest time,
He's drunk on wind-fall apple wine,
It is his favourite season.

He wears a black and yellow vest,
That vicious, beastly, spiteful pest!
He thinks he looks so cute.
But evil deeds are on his mind,
His intentions are all unkind,
The foul, sadistic brute.

And when you picnic in the park,
He'll go along, just for a lark,
To hover round the bin.
Then when you take your litter there,
He'll sting your hand without a care,
Just as you drop it in.

Mid-winter is the safest time.
I'll go outdoors, and feel sublime,
For Waspie is not there.
But when the springtime comes around,
The air fills with his buzzing sound...
I THINK HE'S IN MY HAIR!

Grandma's Hearing Aid

You'll have to speak up...

My grandma lost her hearing, in the twilight of her years.
In order to be heard, I had to SHOUT into her ears.
She didn't think that she was deaf, she'd frown at me and grumble,
"There's nothing wrong with my hearing, it's you young ones - you mumble!"

I finally persuaded her to get a hearing aid,
She wasn't very willing, what a lot of fuss she made!
She didn't want to wear one – hearing aids were for the old.
I said, "Grandma, you're 98, now please, do as you're told!"

The hearing aid was tiny, and fit snugly in her ear,
Not like those great big ear-trumpets they used in yesteryear!
It had a little volume switch, to make it quiet or loud,
To tune if talking one to one, or in a noisy crowd.
I thought my grandma's hearing problems were now at an end.
But little did I know – that thing would drive me round the bend!

Some days I'd get the feeling I was talking to myself,
Then realise the hearing aid was sitting on the shelf.
Or sometimes she would wear it, but forget to turn it on,
Or put it in, then find out that the battery had gone.
Some days it would emit a very high pitched, piercing whine,
Or transmit local radio, *"It's Golden Oldie Time!"*

When we went to a wedding, and the groom had said his part,
From Grandma's left ear, blasted out the song *"Your Cheatin' Heart."*
And one day at the library, she'd fallen fast asleep,
Resounding from her hearing aid, I heard *"Read 'em and Weep."*

My grandma died soon after that, it made me feel so sad.
Her funeral was very grand, the best one to be had.
So at the crematorium, I said my last goodbyes,
And from inside the coffin, I heard *"Smoke Gets in Your Eyes."*

Hell Hath No Fury

Revenge is a dish best served cold...

When I went out to do some shopping,
Just the other week,
A man I used to know came up
And pecked me on the cheek.
It was my ex-fiancé, Bill,
Who dumped me years before!
He broke my poor old heart in two,
And smashed it on the floor.
I've married someone else since then,
A man who's good and kind,
Yet memories of that heartache
Still linger in my mind.

"Hello!" Bill said, "Remember me?
It's been the longest time!
You haven't changed a bit, you know,
You really look sublime!"
"Hello," I said,
"I almost didn't recognise you there,
Perhaps because you've put on weight,
And lost a lot of hair."

We chatted for a minute,
Then I said I had to go.
"Please let me drive you home," Bill said,
"It's chilly out, you know.
And maybe we could take a detour,
Just for old time's sake,
And park up in our favourite place,
Which overlooks the lake."

I pondered for a little while,
And then I said, "OK,
It would be nice to revisit the lakeside,
On the way."
We walked across the parking lot,
To where he'd left his car,
It looked like an expensive one,
A flashy Jaguar.

We drove up to the lakeside,
And Bill parked in our old place,
I recognised desire
Written all across his face.

Bill said, "Let's take a stroll
Out to that clearing, by the trees,
I could bring along a blanket..."
"OK," I smiled, "Yes please!"
Bill jumped out of the car,
And then my hands began to shake,
As stealthily, I reached across
And disengaged the brake...

I got out of the Jag,
And went to follow my ex-love,
And as I passed behind the car,
I gave it quite a shove.
I joined my ex, who gazed at me,
His eyes were filled with hope.
He never even noticed
As his car rolled down the slope.

And as Bill's hands caressed my face
All over, like a rash,
From somewhere close behind us both,
We heard a massive *SPLASH!*
Bill turned around to look,
Then gasped, and did a double take,
When he saw his beloved car
Was floating in the lake!

"My car!" he yelled,
"I'm sure I put the brake on like I oughta,
So how come it went down the slope,
And landed in the water?"

Bill ran down to the water's edge,
Whimpering like a fool,
And kicking both his trainers off,
He jumped into the pool.
Bill grabbed hold of the car's bumper,
And tried to drag it out.
"Don't just stand there,
Come here and help me, quick!" I heard him shout.

"Oh, what a shame!" I sweetly said,
"But please don't make a fuss.
Don't worry how you'll drive me home –
I'll just hop on a bus!"
And with a wave, I walked away,
And left Bill standing there,
Shivering in dirty water,
With wet leaves in his hair.

And as I left I shouted out,
"Consider yourself warned,
To never underestimate
A woman who's been scorned!"

Bloody Hell!

My dad's catchphrase...

My dad was not a patient man,
He often used to curse.
When he became exasperated
He could be quite terse.
There was one phrase he used to shout
At least ten times a day,
When I heard it, I knew that I
Should keep out of his way.

"Bloody Hell!" he cried, when he had dropped the hammer on his thumb.
"Bloody Hell!" he said, when he received a nagging from my mum.
"Bloody Hell!" because the dog had done a whoopsie in the house.
"Bloody Hell!" when Jess the cat bought him a present, of a mouse.

"Bloody Hell!" meant the electric bill was bigger than he thought.
"Bloody Hell!" when he could not locate the item that he sought.
"Bloody Hell!" because the parcel he had ordered didn't come.
"Bloody Hell!" that time an angry donkey bit him on the bum.

My dad's been dead these sixteen years,
Yet I still hear him swear,
When *I* become annoyed,
Then it sounds just like *he* is there!
His grave is in the churchyard,
In a corner plot he lays.
And carved upon his headstone,
There is just one simple phrase -
"Bloody Hell!"

The Guitar

Eric Clapton and Jimi Hendrix have a lot to answer for…

My husband has a guitar,
It is his favourite thing,
He'll polish it on Sundays,
And tighten up the strings.
Then when he's in the middle
Of strumming out a tune,
He pulls such funny faces,
He looks a proper loon!
His eyes glaze over, in his mind
He's at the Albert Hall,
I'm glad he's wearing headphones,
Or he'd drive me up the wall.

Epitaphs

It's very sad when someone dies...

Here's to the memory of John McDeers,
Who worked as a butcher for 21 years.
He fell in the machine that minced up the meat,
And all that was left were the shoes off his feet.

Here lies the body of Teddy McVape,
Whose car was in quite bad mechanical shape.
He went for a drive to the White Cliffs of Dover,
His brakes wouldn't work, and poor Ted went right over.

Here lies the body of Amy McPat,
Who ate too much and grew enormously fat.
She ate 90 donuts, so calorie-loaded,
Her stomach gave out, and poor Amy exploded.

Here lies the body of Katy McFlynn,
Who went on a diet, and grew much too thin.
She went for a walk, as it started to rain,
She stepped in a puddle, and slipped down a drain.

Here lies the body of Toby McFly,
Whose terrible flatulence caused him to die.
He farted too near to the fire one day,
And caused an explosion that blew him away.

Ted's Love Machine

Ted is driven to distraction...

Ted thought that it was time to get a brand new set of wheels.
He'd heard 'The Motor Warehouse' had been offering good deals.
He went along to have a browse at all the cars on show,
He'd been saving up for months, so he had plenty of dough.
He saw a yellow sporty car, and one with alloy rims,
A green one with a sunshine roof, and two with leather trims.
Just as Ted was trying to think which car he liked the most,
A salesman in a suit arrived, and he began to boast.

"Good day, Sir! In our store you'll find the finest cars around,
And I am sure that Sir can spot a bargain, I'll be bound!
What kind of car do you require? What would be your pleasure?
Do you want a car for work, or should it be for leisure?
Perhaps you are a family man, who needs a car that's roomy?
Or maybe you like hip-hop, and want speakers that are boomy?

Could Sir be an outdoors type, who needs a sturdy roof rack?
Or do you own a large dog, who travels in the hatchback?
Do you drive out in all terrains, through rivers, fields and hills?
Or do you stay home when it rains, and practice indoor skills?
Whatever Sir would like to do, whatever your requirement,
I'll find the perfect car for you – or my name's not Bob Finement!"

Poor Ted, he was quite overawed at this flash salesman's patter,
He felt a little sweaty, and his teeth began to chatter.
He pulled himself together, as he tried to find the words.
Then finally he said, "I want a car to pull the birds!"

The salesman gave a knowing smile, and showing all his teeth,
Said, "Sir, I've just the car for you, perfect beyond belief!"
He grabbed Ted's arm, and took him to a shiny blood-red car,
The car was long, and low, and sleek, the sexiest by far.
Ted thought this was the nicest car that he had ever seen,
He knew at once that he had found the perfect *love machine!*

The salesman said, "This vehicle will fulfil your wildest dreams.
When you drive down the street in this, you'll hear the women's screams!
The engine goes from nought to *PHWOAR,* faster than a wink.
It has on-board computers, so you don't need to think.
The controls are voice activated, you won't have to shout.
There's a thing that lights cigars, and there's one that stubs them out.
It has MP3 and wi-fi, and cruise control functions,
A thing to change traffic lights, when stuck at busy junctions.

The interior's upholstered in finest calf-skin leather,
With heated seats and air con, so you'll never mind the weather.

The seats fold down into a bed, in case you want a nap.
Or if you like, the satnav has a Kama Sutra app!
There's a mini bar, a mirror ball, and a condom machine.
(It is best to play it safe, in case you don't know where she's been!)
Now Sir, come with me, and we'll negotiate the price,
And I'll even throw in complementary furry dice!"

So Ted went with the salesman, though it seemed rather rash,
And meekly handed over his hard-earned pile of cash.
And as he drove away in his brand new shiny motor,
He spotted, walking down the street, Katy Ann Dakota.

Now Ted had fancied Katy Ann since he was a young lad.
He'd always wished to ask her out, but so far, never had.
Deciding he would chance it, he pulled over to the side,
And rolling down the window, said, "Do you fancy a ride?"
Katy looked down at the car, and with a charming smile,
Said, "Blimey, you know how to drive a girl around in style!"
She got into the car, and then they zoomed off down the street.
Ted felt so glad he'd bought the car, it suited him a treat!

He knew just where he was going, he drove to Lover's Hill.
Ted stopped the car, then leaned across, and moved in for the kill.
Romantic music filled the air, the lights were soft and low,
The leather seats reclining back, as far as they would go.
With champagne from the mini bar, and aphrodisiac food,
The mirror ball rotated, just to get them in the mood.
Ted was so excited, and his mind was in a whirl.
He leant across to kiss her – at last he'd got his girl!
But as their passion grew, and the windows began to steam,
Disaster struck! Alas, poor Ted did not fulfil his dream.

Suddenly, the power went! The car grew quiet and still.
The heat went off, and Kate began to shiver in the chill.
"What's happening?" asked Katy. "What the bloody hell was that?"
But Ted knew only too well – the battery had gone flat!

The romantic mood evaporated - passion killed, stone dead.
Katy Ann pulled away, and shot a withering look at Ted.
Katy said, "Ted, you're a joke! I think that we should part.
Take me home at once!" He said, "I can't, the car won't start!"
"Ted, that's no way to treat a girl, that takes the cake, it does!
I s'pose I'll have to walk home now, or catch the bloody bus!"
Katy climbed out of the car, and the door closed with a slam.
She ran off down the road, and jumped aboard a passing tram.

Poor Ted was left all alone, hot tears fell into his lap.
He wished he'd never bought the car – expensive pile of crap!
He got his mobile phone out, and gave Finement a call.
He said, "You'll have to tow this car, for it's no use at all!"
Ted said, "I want a refund, I want all my money back,
And if you try to argue, I'll make sure you get the sack!"

So the salesman fetched the car, and gave the money back to Ted.
Now Ted hasn't got a car, he rides a bicycle instead.

Spider, spider

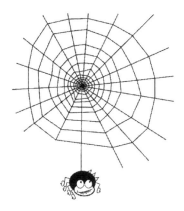

If you have eight legs, you're not coming in...

Spider, spider in my garden,
On your web so fine.
Spinning threads of finest silk,
Small insects to entwine.

Though you're welcome in my garden,
Please don't be misled.
If you come inside my house,
You'll end up squashed, and dead.

Today Is Not a Good Day

Just one of those days...

Today is not a good day,
I overslept this morning,
I got to work ten minutes late,
Bleary eyed, and yawning.
The boss gave me a telling off,
And what made matters worse,
He made me work all through my lunch,
Oh, how he made me curse!

Today is not a good day,
The heel came right off my shoe,
I had to stick in on again,
With chewing gum and glue.
It broke again two hours later,
When running for the bus.
I fell into a puddle!
But I didn't make a fuss.

Today is not a good day,
I do feel rather unwell.
It may be something serious,
It's difficult to tell.
My head hurts, and my nose runs,
And my muscles really ache.
There's purple spots across my chest,
My skin's begun to flake!

Today is not a good day,
My boyfriend upped and left,
He's found another woman,
And I am all bereft.
He met her in the fishmonger's,
While buying some red snapper.
Well, they're welcome to each other -
Him and his big fat slapper!

Today is not a good day,
The postman didn't come,
I didn't get one parcel,
Not even from my mum.
But why did that upset me so,
And fill me with dismay?
I'd rather hoped for something,
'Cause *today is my birthday!*

Today is not a good day,
There is no food in the house,
Except a little piece of cheese,
That wouldn't feed a mouse.

Monday has been rather horrid,
It really must be said.
If Tuesday's going to be the same,
I'm staying home, in bed!

Fair-Weather Friend

What are friends for?

I've *so* much work to do today,
I could use your assistance.
I've done all I can do alone,
Through hard work and persistence.
I helped do your work last week,
You did not struggle alone.
You say that you don't want to help?
I'll manage on my own.

I really feel quite ill today,
I'm in a lot of pain.
Like when you were ill last month,
And I brought soup, in the rain.

You say that you don't want to come
And nurse me back to health?
Ok, don't give another thought,
I'll look after myself.

I'm feeling very sad today,
A relative has died.
Remember when your grandpa passed?
I held you as you cried.
You say you're having too much fun
To hear me cry and moan?
Ok, well you enjoy yourself,
I'll get through it alone.

Hooray! I've won the lottery!
I thought I'd let you know.
As soon as I receive the cash,
Around the world I'll go!
What's that you say? You'll go with me,
Wherever I may roam?
Don't bother, I don't need your help,
I'll spend it on my own!

Would Like to Meet

Profiles on online dating sites can be misleading...

I'd been single for a while,
So I thought I'd like to meet
A lovely handsome fella,
Who would sweep me off my feet.
I had a go at speed dating,
But it wasn't for me,
The men I met were boring,
And one guy was eighty-three!
I went to a few singles nights,
But without much success,
There was one man who asked me out –
But he was in a dress!

And then a friend suggested
That I join a dating site.
She said, "They'll match your profile,
So you could meet Mister Right!"

And so I joined *'Would Like To Meet'.*
Filled out the online profile,
With questions like 'what colour eyes?'
And 'are you fierce, or docile?'
I uploaded a photo,
(One that made me look quite young!)
Then waited for some messages.
It didn't take too long.

I had quite a few emails,
Though some of them seemed weird,
One had tattoos on his face,
And one had a pink beard!
But then I got an email
From a very handsome man,
We shared a lot of interests,
He said his name was Dan.
We exchanged several messages,
And chatted on the phone.
I felt that I had met 'the one' –
I need not be alone!

So we arranged a rendezvous
Where Dan and I could meet.
I got there a bit early,
And looked up and down the street.
I gazed around for handsome Dan,
So tall and slim and dark,
But no one fitted that description,
Standing near the park.

The only person waiting
Was a short, fat, hairless man,
Holding a bunch of roses,
Leaning up against a van.

Maybe Dan was running late?
I *was* a little early,
Then the short, fat fella said,
"Hello, you must be Shirley!"
I stared at him in horror,
This chap wasn't my dream man!
He seemed to read my thoughts,
He said, "Hello, it's me, I'm Dan."

I said, "I've been misled!
I thought you were tall, slim and dark!"
He said, "I know,
I used a photo of my best friend, Mark.
I thought if I was honest,
Then you wouldn't want to know.
But now that we're both here,
Well, shall we just give it a go?"

"OK," I said, "I might as well,
I've nothing else to do."
He said, "I've booked a table
At that restaurant, 'Taboo'".
We went on to the restaurant,
The food was very nice,
Dan insisted that he would pay,
Regardless of the price.

He paid me every compliment,
He made me feel so fine,
I felt a little giddy,
And it wasn't just the wine!
He made me feel appreciated,
Special, like a lady.
He had such perfect manners,
And he didn't slurp his gravy!

I was rather bowled over
By his flattery and charm,
And when we left the restaurant,
We walked home arm in arm.
He asked if we could meet again,
And so I said, "Yes please!"
(Though when we kissed goodnight,
I had to bend down at the knees!)

Since then, we've been on lots of dates,
Dan's such a perfect gent.
He pays me loads of compliments,
They're all sincerely meant.
I soon began to realise
That though Dan's only small,
In terms of personality,
He's over six feet tall!

He may not be a looker,
But he's perfect in my eyes,
I wanted a dream fella,
And I think I've won the prize.

So if you're feeling lonely,
And want to find a lover,
Bear one thing in mind –
'Never judge a book by its cover'.

The Annoying Fly

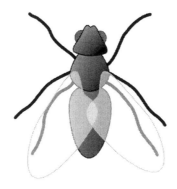

Flies are not easy to get rid of...

The fly is an annoying beast,
He buzzes round my head,
And whistles past my ear
When I am tucked up in my bed.

And when he's in my kitchen,
Well, his habits are quite rude!
He spreads his foul germs everywhere,
And craps upon my food.

So if a fly gets in your home,
And you wish to stay healthy,
Grab a rolled up newspaper,
And creep up on him, so stealthy.

Just when he does not suspect
Your tabloid-wielding caper,
Bring your hand down really quick,
And swat him with the paper!

Then as you scrutinize the floor
For his blood-stained remains,
He'll buzz right past your face,
And you will have to try again.

The 1970's

It was a fab and funky time...

I grew up in the 70's,
A wonderful decade!
With Chopper bikes and Space Hoppers,
And Alpine lemonade.
We dressed in flares, and platform shoes,
And collars long and wide,
With hair done in a feather-cut,
All flicked back at the side.

I used to spend my pocket money
Buying loads of sweets,
Spangles, Toffo's, Marathons,
Opal Fruits and Peanut Treats.

When Marathon was changed to Snickers,
They seemed to get smaller.
Or are they really the same size –
It's just me that's grown taller?

Home furnishings were bright and bold,
With colours loud and clashing,
And busy patterned wallpapers,
With fabrics that weren't matching.
Our carpet - orange, blue and green,
In nylon shag, so thick,
You couldn't stare at it too long,
Or it made you feel sick!

Pop music was exciting,
We had Glam, Disco and Funk.
Before the Silver Jubilee,
We saw the birth of Punk.
I'd tune to The Top Forty,
On our old Bush radio,
And on TV, Top of the Pops
Was the best music show.

We only had three channels
On our black and white TV.
Channel 2 just showed the test card,
All day till half past three.
But when the kids' programmes came on,
We'd be glued to the box,
With shows like Bagpuss, Fingerbobs,
And Basil Brush, the fox.

The picture wasn't very clear,
It used to roll and jump,
Though sometimes you could cure it,
If you gave the set a thump.
Or move the aerial around,
Up, down, then side to side -
We had to hold it in the air
While watching Nationwide!

I once asked Jim'll Fix It
To fulfil a dream for me,
To meet with Gary Glitter,
Rolf Harris and D.L.T.
I never got an answer,
I felt so let-down and sad,
But now we know they're sex-pests,
Well, I'm really rather glad!

It was a busy era
For industrial unrest,
With power cuts, and bakers' strikes
To put us to the test.
We had to sit in candle light,
And bake all our own bread.
Then when ITV went on strike,
Watched BBC instead.

These modern times aren't so much fun
As when I was a nipper!
We've only got the internet,
Facebook, Youtube and Twitter,

Recordable cable TV,
Playstations, home PC's,
Search engines, apps and Ipads,
Spotify and MP3's.
3D movies, online shops,
Smartphones, to text or call,
Shop-bought bread, no power cuts...
Can't grumble, after all!

Urban Garden Dwellers

Meet the creatures who live on your doorstep...

I am an urban fox,
I often hang around your bin,
I like to have my dinner there,
When you put food scraps in.
And when I've finished dining,
If I remain unseen,
I'll leave a pile of droppings,
Just so you know I've been.

I am a robin red-breast,
So colourful and cute.
You'll hear me in the garden,
I whistle like a flute.

I like to eat insects and worms,
But when the ground gets hard,
I've got a nice little sideline -
I pose for Christmas cards!

I am a garden tortoise,
And I potter slowly round.
I never travel very far,
I don't cover much ground.
The other creatures mock me,
And they criticize my pace.
They don't believe that I once beat
That fast hare, in a race!

I am a naughty squirrel,
Hiding up in a tree.
If your bird-feeder's empty,
It probably was me!
I nip across the garden,
I know all the short cuts,
And when no one is looking,
I pinch the sparrow's nuts!

I am a prickly hedgehog,
I live under the shed.
I've gathered some moss and leaves,
To make a cosy bed.
I wait under the feeder,
Until the squirrel comes.
He's such a messy eater!
So I pick up the crumbs.

I am a little sparrow,
All feathery and brown.
I too live in the garden,
I like it in the town.
I hate that bloody squirrel -
The greedy little bleeder!
I wish a bolt of lightning
Would blast him off my feeder!

Something for the Pain

Just what the doctor ordered...

I rang up the doctor's to make an appointment,
I needed some help, but just got disappointment.
The person who answered said, "Dr Siddique's,
If you're feeling ill, then the wait is three weeks.
If you need a doctor today, you've no chance,
You can't just *be* ill, you must plan in advance!
If it's life and death, then go to A&E,
Get there before nine, you'll be seen by half-three."

I wasn't quite dying, so I had to wait,
I went three weeks later, at quarter past eight.
An hour later, and I still sat and waited,
I'd rushed to get there, so I felt quite frustrated!
I got rather angry, I was fit to burst,
For others came later, and they went in first!

I needed a wee, it was starting to burn,
But knew if I went, that I might miss my turn.
The seats were rock hard, and back pain is my trouble,
I knew when I left there, my pain would be double!
When finally I was called into his room,
The doctor looked up, and surveyed me with gloom.
It's not very often I get one that's nice,
And rarely do I see the same doctor twice!

The doctor said grumpily, "What brings you here?"
I said, "I've had back pain for over a year."
He said, "Paracetamol, four times a day."
I said, "I've tried that, but the pain's here to stay."
He sighed, and said, "Well, climb up on that high couch."
I said, "Gis a leg up, I'm not Peter Crouch!"
He prodded my back, and said, "Where's the pain worst?"
His hands were like ice – why don't they warm them first?
I said, "It hurts all round the base of my spine,
And nothing helps, except a bottle of wine."

He said, "What you need is an MRI scan,
An osteopath, and a pain treatment plan.
But there is no funding for them anymore,
So take ibuprofen, and sleep on the floor.
If that doesn't help, there's no more I can do.
I've fifty more patients to see after you!"

So I went back home, and I got out the Pinot,
And treated my back with a large glass of vino.
I'll use that as medicine, regular doses.
It's better than pain killers, or self-hypnosis!

It's easy to get, unlike doctor's prescriptions,
With NHS red tape, and funding restrictions.
A few years from now, here is my diagnosis,
I'll be down the doctor's with liver cirrhosis!

And though heavy drinking may not seem too clever,
It's medical fact that no one lives forever.
So since death is something there is no avoidin',
There's no point in worrying – so pick your poison!

The Online Auction Site

Ebay can be quite addictive...

I joined an online auction site
A month or two ago.
I'd heard it was a clever way
To make some extra dough.
My house was full of clutter,
And I needed to get rid.
I thought I could create some space,
While earning a few quid.

I sorted out the spare room,
And found my old treadmill.
I'd bought it hoping to get fit –
But it just made me ill!
I found a pile of comics,
And some clothes that didn't fit.
Well, all of those could go,
And I might earn a little bit.

I went up to the attic,
And found some baby things,
Bags of clothes and teddies,
Feeding cups and teething rings.
Well, all of those could go,
My parenting days are done.
My children are grown up now,
They've left home and moved on.

I went into the kitchen,
And I had a poke around.
I knew that in there
Lots of unused gadgets would be found.
There was a yogurt maker,
And a bread making machine,
A fancy cocktail shaker,
And an oversized tureen.
I've never even used them,
They're brand new in the box.
And whatever made me purchase
Three electric woks?

I went down to the garden shed,
And found a painting kit,
Which promised you could decorate,
And make light work of it.
It's supposed to paint a ceiling,
Without making a mess.
But when I tried, the paint ran down my arm,
And down my dress!

I found some more old bric-a-brac,
And some assorted tat,
A set of rusty golf clubs,
And an ugly china cat.
I listed them all on the site,
And watched the bids roll in!
I felt so glad I hadn't
Chucked the lot into the bin.

Then when the auctions ended,
And the buyers had all paid,
I posted all the items.
What a lot of cash I'd made!
My home had loads of extra space,
It seemed a whole lot bigger.
And when I checked my bank balance,
I saw a healthy figure!

But then I started browsing
Around the auction site,
At other people's listings,
Some sounded quite alright...

I placed a bid on someone's
Part worn exercise machine,
A *pre-loved* ice cream maker,
And a *vintage* Chinese screen.
A pile of books, some CD's,
And a 1960's lamp,
A limited edition disc
Of Lady and the Tramp,

A pair of shoes, a dress or two,
A thing to trim a beard...
And very soon, my new-found space
Completely disappeared!

My house has been *re-cluttered!*
Oh, how could I be so rash?
I'll have to have another sale –
I'm nearly out of cash!

Getting Older

It comes to us all...

It seems like only yesterday that I was young and free,
My whole life to look forward to, with all that I could be.
But now I'm almost 50, and my best years have all passed.
It seemed to go so quickly - how can time move on so fast?

I used to have such lovely hair, long flowing chestnut locks,
But now it seems much thinner, and the colour's from a box.
I have to dye it so often, to cover my grey roots,
I must have paid a fortune out, to L'Oreal and Boots!

I used to be so slender, I was only skin and bone,
Now if I walk past a cake shop, I put on half a stone.
As I've got older, gravity has seemed to grow much stronger,
For everything's begun to droop, my face seems rather longer.

So now if I'm not smiling, both my cheeks hang down and sag,
Which makes me look quite grumpy, like a bad-tempered old hag!
But when I smile at people, though my eyes still shine and twinkle,
The skin around them creases up into one great big wrinkle!

If I look in the mirror now, it's not myself I see,
Instead I see my mother, standing staring back at me.
Unless I have been drinking, and have a bad hangover,
I look less like my mom then - more like our bloodhound, Rover!

Once, I had so much energy, I'd leap right out of bed,
But now when I wake up, I groan, and feel like I'm half dead.
My body aches so much, just getting up each day is hard,
Good thing I'm not a horse – they'd send me to the knacker's yard!

When I was young, I dreamed that I would dance with Legs and Co,
And be on TV every week, on that pop music show.
My dream didn't come true, my dance career was not to be,
If I tried dancing now, I'd just end up in A&E!

Now old age is beckoning, false teeth and hip replacement.
It comes to each one of us, we mustn't get complacent.
Enjoy yourself while you are young, and do not hesitate,
Before you know it you'll be old, and it will be too late!

Do all the things you want to do, take chances and be bold,
At least then you'll have no regrets, when you are grey and old.
Then when you're on your Zimmer frame, or in your walk-in bath,
You'll look back on your life and say, "At least I had a laugh!"

Although my body's getting on, I feel quite young inside,
I still want to have a giggle, not sit at home and hide.
And even when I'm ninety, I'll act silly and playful,
I won't be mature and wise - I'll be old and disgraceful!

My Garden

Weed it and reap...

How I love my garden!
I can potter round for hours,
Pruning back the roses,
And dead-heading all the flowers.
I'll mow the lawn, and pull the weeds,
And irrigate the border.
Then trim along the ivy,
Just to keep it all in order.

I'll sweep the path, and paint the fence,
And fertilize the plants.
Then I'll just sit and watch a line
Of busy worker ants.
The bumble bee amazes me,
As he buzzes about,
Visiting each pretty flower,
To suck the nectar out.

If I sit still, the birds will come.
They know they'll get a feed,
All pecking at their table,
For the little grains of seed.
A hedgehog ambles past the shed,
Snuffling the ground.
And gaily patterned butterflies,
Flutter all around.

So when I'm in my garden,
Please don't visit me, or phone,
I'll probably ignore you,
Or pretend that no one's home.
And on the day that I die,
Please don't cry, or make a din.
Just take me down the garden,
Shove me in the compost bin.

An Infinite Number of Monkeys

Everyone needs to take a break...

An infinite number of monkeys were locked in a room.
Well, most of them were monkeys, there was also one baboon.
They gave them all a typewriter, and set them all to work.
Without even a lunch break, they were not allowed to shirk!

The monkeys started typing, and then after quite a while,
The baboon started writing stuff in old Will Shakespeare's style.
He typed, "To be, or not to be," but then he sat quite still.
The organisers scratched their heads, they thought that he was ill.

But all the baboon needed was to have a cup of tea,
And eat a nice banana, stretch his legs, and have a wee.
He only wanted half an hour – a quick break, and a munch,
Well, even Mister Shakespeare must have stopped to have some lunch!

The Empty Page

Writer's block is no joke…

I want to write a poem,
But my brain will not comply.
The empty page is taunting me,
I struggle and I sigh.

I can't think of a subject,
If I do, it doesn't rhyme.
I sit and stare, the clock ticks on,
How slowly goes the time!

And then an idea comes to me,
I seize the paper – bingo!
I fold it like an aeroplane,
And throw it out the window.

21 Years

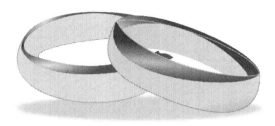

It's a life sentence...

For 21 years, we've been husband and wife,
He is my 'Old Man', I'm his 'Worry and Strife'.
Like most couples, we've had our fair share of troubles,
Sometimes life's a prick, and will burst all your bubbles.
Yes, sometimes our problems have caused us to curse,
But on the whole, I'd say things could have been worse.

Our shared sense of humour began our romance,
Although that was tested, when I saw him dance!
Our laughter's the glue that has kept us together,
And helped us to cope through the spells of bad weather.
We made some mistakes, but we're much wiser now,
We've learned to avoid things that might cause a row.

So I don't pick flies when he does DIY,
Though our shelves are crooked, at least he did try!
And if I've been painting, and I've missed a bit,
He knows he should just keep quiet about it!

And one fact has been made abundantly clear,
I *must not* suggest a day out at IKEA!
And he knows the last thing that I want to do,
Is spend the day browsing around B&Q!

He's often quite grumpy first thing in the morning,
He could bite my head off, without any warning.
But he puts up with me when I am in a mood,
And he never complains when I burn all his food.
His untidiness gets me in a right tizz,
If there's stuff on the floor, it's usually his.
But he puts up with all my whinging and moaning,
And incessant chatter, without even groaning.

It's not just the two of us now, we've a daughter,
We strive to protect her, come hell or high water.
She's 18 years old, and so clever and witty,
Hardworking and sensible, charming and pretty.
She's nothing like us! And I wonder, just maybe,
If when she was born, we brought home the wrong baby?

Once romance meant presents, and chocolates and flowers,
And candle lit dinners, and talking for hours.
But now we prefer to watch TV instead,
And eat chocolate biscuits and Pringles in bed!
When my back is itching, he'll give it a scratch,
And I'll pluck his ears, while he's watching the match.

We're both getting fatter, and greyer, and older,
I've got a bad back, and he's got a bad shoulder.

I have hot flushes, and fibromyalgia,
He gets reflux, flatulence and neuralgia.
It's fair to say neither of us is a catch,
We're both knackered – at least we make a good match!

So as we move onward down life's rocky path,
Whatever happens, we'll make each other laugh.
And when we get old, and our flesh starts to sag,
We'll help change each other's colostomy bag!
He will look after me, and I'll be his nurse,
That's what marriage is for, for better or worse.
A faithful companion is worth more than wealth,
For richer, for poorer, in sickness and health.

Home Maintenance

It never ends...

In my house, there are *always* jobs that need doing,
A ceiling needs painting, a loose shelf needs screwing.
A roof tile is missing, the gutter is sagging,
The bath sealant's gone, and the pipes all need lagging.
The brickwork needs pointing, the shed roof still leaks -
I fixed that, but it only lasted three weeks!

The toilet won't flush, as the ball-cock has broke,
The bath has gone rusty, I can't have a soak.
The sitting room needs to be redecorated,
The paintwork is chipped, and the wallpaper's dated.
The bedroom and bathroom doors both need re-hanging,
The kitchen tap drips, and the window keeps banging.

It's not that I'm lazy, or don't want to bother,
But soon as I do one job, up pops another!

And nothing's straightforward, or ever goes right,
I start a quick task, and it takes me all night!
When I did the bedroom, I had *such* a caper,
The plaster all came off, along with the paper!

And nothing I buy ever works as it should,
I bought some emulsion, and that was no good.
They said, "It's hardwearing, and easily wiped,"
The paint wiped right off – so the wall now looks striped!
The bookcase I bought came without half the screws.
The new doormat shredded when I wiped my shoes.

Home ownership's not all it's cracked up to be,
It's not worth the hassle, you take it from me.
If you need a home, here's advice, kindly meant,
Don't bother with property – live in a tent!

Autumn Leaves

Autumn is not all mists and mellow fruitfulness...

In Autumn, leaves blow everywhere,
Around my feet, and in my hair.
Although their colours might impress,
Good grief, they don't half make a mess!
They're dry and crunchy, for a time,
But when they're wet, they turn to slime.
So walk with caution on damp grass,
Or else you'll end up on your ass!

Each time I open my front door,
A pile of leaves drifts on my floor.
Just like a dirty brown snowfall,
They litter my once tidy hall.
I have to sweep them all away
About a hundred times a day!

The Summer gave us flowers, fair,
Now Autumn's trash lies everywhere.
A messy garden's not my style,
I rake the leaves into a pile,
I put the rake away, and then -
The wind blows them all back again!

Some poets like to celebrate,
The sight the Autumn leaves create.
But I prefer them when they're green,
Trees covered with a verdant screen.
Autumn means the year is dying,
Leaves fall like tears, trees are crying.
Much shorter days, the weather's bad,
And lack of sunshine makes me sad.

So poets, please don't waste my time,
Telling me Autumn is sublime,
Unless you want to feel my wrath,
Go fetch a broom, and sweep my path!

My Cat

An infuriating, furry feline friend...

My pussycat, he drives me mad!
He wakes me up in bed.
When he decides it's breakfast time,
He pounces on my head.
He brings in mice and birds and rats,
Oh, how he makes me shout!
I have to grab a sturdy broom,
To shoo the creatures out.

He scratched my leather chair,
And knocked my best vase off the table.
I'd send him back from whence he came,
If only I was able!
I didn't plan to own a cat,
He just turned up one day.
His old owners had thrown him out,
They said he couldn't stay.

He somehow knew to find my door,
And scratched to be let in.
I saw that he was scrawny,
Fed him tuna, from a tin.

A bowl of milk, a comfy bed,
He soon felt right at home.
A few good meals, he put on weight,
No longer skin and bone.
I gently bathed his weepy eye,
And soothed his poorly paws,
And soon cat treats and kitty toys
Filled up my kitchen drawers.

And now he's such a happy lad!
His coat's so sleek and black.
And even when he's naughty,
I will not give him a smack.
He drives me mad,
But just one look from those green feline eyes,
He makes me want to cuddle him,
And praise him to the skies!

If I ever meet his old owners,
Knowing what they've done,
I'd like to tell them what I think,
And shoot 'em with a gun!
I hope my cat still visits them,
I don't want him to stay,
Just crap all round their garden,
Flick his tail, then walk away.

The Sewing Machine

This is a true story about something strange that happened to me at Halloween....

My mother used to make my clothes,
When I was just a kid.
She bought a small sewing machine,
A 'Singer', for five quid.
She'd make me pretty dresses,
From a length of printed cotton,
Her clever skill and willingness
Will never be forgotten.

Our friends and neighbours all came round,
To have their garments altered,
She always did a perfect job,
Her stitches never faltered.
When I came home from school,
I'd find her at the sewing table,
The Singer running up the seams,
As fast as it was able.

I often wished that I possessed
My mom's sewing prowess,
But when I tried dressmaking,
I just made rather a mess!
My mother used to shake her head,
Then put right what I'd started.
She passed away three years ago.
It left me broken hearted.

I had to sort through her effects,
And found my mom's old Singer.
Around that old sewing machine
Her spirit seemed to linger.
I couldn't bear to part with it,
So kept it for myself.
I took it home, and put it in the attic,
On a shelf.

I didn't think I'd use it,
But just lately I've grown thin.
My clothes had got quite baggy,
And they needed taking in.
I fetched the Singer from the loft,
To see if it still worked.
The motor whirred! The bobbin spun!
The needle never shirked.

The sound of that old Singer
Made my mother seem so near.
Then something spooky happened,
It was really very queer.

I started on my sewing,
Though it wasn't going well.
I wasn't stitching straight,
The seams were crooked, I could tell.
I left the Singer,
While I went to get my mobile phone.
I heard a noise –
The Singer started sewing on its own!
From right across the room,
I watched the Singer whirr and sew,
With no foot on the pedal switch,
To make the motor go.

I ran across the room,
And cut the power at the plug,
Then getting out the Scotch bottle,
I took a healthy slug!
My pulse raced as I thought
About the sight that I had seen.
What unseen force had operated
My mom's old machine?

Had my mother's spirit come back,
To show me how it's done?
Just like she used to do,
To finish off what I'd begun.
Or was it just a power fault
That made the motor go,
While no one was near the machine?
I guess I'll never know.

The Singer's gone back up the loft,
I thought that it was best.
I'll have to buy some new clothes,
If I want to be well dressed!
And if garments hang loose on me,
Because I've grown too svelte,
To make my trousers fit –
Well, I'll just have to wear a belt!

The Night Before Christmas

Santa isn't the only one who works hard at Christmas...

T'was the night before Christmas. Down in the kitchen,
Our mother was swearing and cursing and bitchin'.
"Oh, why is it *me* who must sort it all out?"
She moaned, as she decapitated a sprout.
"I do all the cleaning, and shopping, and cooking.
I wrap all the presents, when no one is looking.
I write all the cards, and put them in the post.
I bake the mince pies, like a good Christmas host.

I put up the tree, and I hang decorations.
I cook Christmas dinner, for all the relations.
I even do everyone else's gift shopping -
They'd only forget. It's no wonder I'm dropping!
And every year, it's exactly the same.
It's really not fair, and I think it's a shame.

At Christmas, it's women who do all the work,
It makes me so angry, it drives me berserk!
Well I've had enough, I can't take any more!"
She stood up, and dropped all the sprouts on the floor.

She went to her laptop, and typed an email,
And sent it to every disgruntled female.
"Dear women, it's time that we stopped being a slave,
Until our families learn how to behave!
Without our hard work, there'd be no Christmas Day!
I'm calling a strike! Ladies, what do you say?"

So all of the women downed tools right away,
As soon as they read Mother's communiqué.
They all left their homes, walked out into the night.
So on Christmas morning, when it became light,
The families woke up to no smell of cooking.
No sign of the women, although they went looking.
No presents to open, and no decorations,
And no tasty food, for yuletide celebrations.

The families didn't know what to say,
"Where is our Mum? And where's our Christmas Day?
Not one of the nice things that make Christmas fun
Have happened this year - why has nothing been done?"
So they all sat down, and they tried hard to think,
Why Mother was not in her place, at the sink.
And after a while they all started to see,
It was overwork that had made Mother flee!

"No wonder she's vanished! We should have tried harder,
To help with the shopping, and fill up the larder.
We should have done some of the cooking and cleaning,
To make Mother do it all was so demeaning!
We should have helped out with the presents and cards,
We let Mother do it all, that was too hard!

We all had fun, while she did all the labour,
Now we're ashamed of our selfish behaviour.
From now on we'll make sure we all do our share,
Give Mother a break, for it seems only fair.
She should be allowed to enjoy Christmas too,
Relax, put her feet up, with nothing to do."

So the families sent an emphatic text,
"Mothers, please come home! We no longer expect
That you should do all of the festive hard work,
We've all been so selfish, we've all been a jerk!
Come home and relax, you'll have no work to do.
For this year, we're all going to wait upon YOU!"

So the women went home, and they sat in a chair,
While their families cooked lunch, and ran here and there,
Wrapping all the presents, and trimming the tree.
While mothers relaxed, and surveyed them with glee.

So this festive season, you know what to do.
Please let your poor mother enjoy Christmas too!

The Secret of Happiness

It's no big mystery...

What's the secret of happiness?
It's little things, I guess,
Like when you go out shopping,
And you find the ideal dress.

The perfect cup of coffee,
Just before you face the day.
Discovering that lost receipt
You thought you'd thrown away.

Your missing cat returning home,
From four days on the prowl.
The singing of a robin,
Or the hooting of an owl.

Finding out your visa bill
Is less than you expected.
Hearing your job application
Hasn't been rejected.

Moonlit walks along a beach,
Or sunshine after rain.
Watching fluffy snowflakes
Drifting past the window pane.

A DJ plays your favourite song,
A letter from a friend,
Or reading a new book
That keeps you gripped right to the end.

The wagging of a puppy's tail,
The laughter of a child.
Discovering a precious orchid
Growing in the wild.

Standing upon the scale,
To find you've lost a pound or two.
Remembering your library books,
Before they're overdue.

Getting there right on time,
When you feared you would be late.
Someone who you always fancied
Asks you for a date.

The scent of autumn bonfires,
The first daffodils in spring.
A solitary skylark,
Who is calling on the wing.

The hairdresser who cuts your hair
Exactly how you said.
Discovering your guinea pig is just asleep,
Not dead.

The suit that is a perfect fit,
The train that comes on time.
Finding money you'd forgotten,
Or hearing church bells chime.

Opening your birthday cards,
Shared laughter with a friend.
Hearing a sick relative
At last is on the mend.

Finding some expensive shoes
Reduced to half the price.
Somebody who notices
When you are looking nice.

The traffic light that stayed on green,
The toast that wasn't burnt.
The customer who always pays on time,
What you have earned.

Cider on a summer's day,
Hot cocoa, when it's cold.
Finding out the house you wanted
Hasn't yet been sold.

The important piece of paper
You remembered to keep.
The telephone that didn't ring
While baby was asleep.

The TV that broke down
Before the guarantee expired.
The welcome of a comfy bed,
When you are feeling tired.

Whatever life may throw at you,
Whatever fortune brings,
Be sure to count your blessings,
And enjoy the little things.

The End.

Thank you for reading my book. If you enjoyed it,
I hope you will take a moment to leave a review with the retailer.
It would be very much appreciated!

Viv Wade.

About the Author

Viv Wade lives in the Black Country area of the West Midlands, England. She has a husband, an 18-year-old daughter, and two cats.

Some of her poems are based on her personal experiences, some are based on observations, and some are completely made-up. Except the one about the love machine, and the one about the fart-powered plane. Those things really happened...

When she is not writing, her hobbies include avoiding people with clipboards, scowling at politicians on TV, and tutting in queues.